TAMING AND TRAINING YOUR
FIRST BUDGERIGAR
KW-070

Contents

Photographers: Dr. Herbert R. Axelrod, H. Bielfeld, Michael Gilroy, A. Jesse, Harry V. Lacey, R. and V. Moat, H. Reinhard, Vince Serbin, Louise Van der Meid, Norma Veitch, Vogelpark Walsrode, Wayne Wallace.

Overleaf: The author training one of her budgies. **Title page:** Training budgies can be a fun, rewarding experience for both the owner and the pet.

© 1988 by T.F.H. Publications, Inc.

Distributed in the UNITED STATES by T.F.H. Publications, Inc., One T.F.H. Plaza, Neptune City, NJ 07753; in CANADA to the Pet Trade by H & L Pet Supplies Inc., 27 Kingston Crescent, Kitchener, Ontario N2B 2T6; Rolf C. Hagen Ltd., 3225 Sartelon Street, Montreal 382 Quebec; in CANADA to the Book Trade by Macmillan of Canada (A Division of Canada Publishing Corporation), 164 Commander Boulevard, Agincourt, Ontario M1S 3C7; in ENGLAND by T.F.H. Publications Limited, Cliveden House/Priors Way/Bray, Maidenhead, Berkshire SL6 2HP, England; in AUSTRALIA AND THE SOUTH PACIFIC by T.F.H. (Australia) Pty. Ltd., Box 149, Brookvale 2100 N.S.W., Australia; in NEW ZEALAND by Ross Haines & Son, Ltd., 18 Monmouth Street, Grey Lynn, Auckland 2, New Zealand; in SINGAPORE AND MALAYSIA by MPH Distributors (S) Pte., Ltd., 601 Sims Drive, #03/07/21, Singapore 1438; in the PHILIPPINES by Bio-Research, 5 Lippay Street, San Lorenzo Village, Makati Rizal; in SOUTH AFRICA by Multipet Pty. Ltd., 30 Turners Avenue, Durban 4001. Published by T.F.H. Publications, Inc. Manufactured in the United States of America by T.F.H. Publications, Inc.

TAMING AND TRAINING
YOUR FIRST BUDGERIGAR

RISA TEITLER
PROFESSIONAL TRAINER

There is a fantastic wealth of literature on the care of budgerigars in captivity. This book is aimed at helping the owner of a first budgie. The correct feeding and maintenance of the bird and the successful taming of it are my primary concerns.

Carefully read the section on how to choose a healthy young budgie and acquire the best possible accessories and feed that you can. The inexpensive, expressive little budgie can become one of your most faithful companions. With proper care and training it will enrich your life for many years.

Respect your budgie and always seek the advice of a qualified vet if you suspect illness, rather than letting its health depond upon the home remedies of well meaning but inexperienced friends. Good luck with your first budgie, the first of many!

Opposite: *The most inexpensive of all parrots is the budgie, a companionable bird that is tamed and trained quite easily.*
Right: *Budgies are capable of becoming very attached to their owners.*

Introduction

The Australian shell parakeet, so called due to the black barring on the wings, is probably the best known of all parrots in captivity. Also known as the budgerigar, this bird inhabits the interior of the Australian continent and lives in large migratory flocks.

Budgerigars are small birds. The total body length is approximately six inches, and adults weigh less than one ounce. In the wild, budgerigars are basically green birds, with yellow facial feathers and long, tapering dark blue tails. In captivity, however, budgies have been bred to many different colors and shades. They are commonly available in all shades of green and blue, yellow (lutino), white, and pied (a mixture of two colors). Prolific breeders, budgies have long been the favorite of aviculturists who employ controlled breeding. Budgies mature quickly and cross freely (from one color to another). They are easy to maintain and are usually good parents, producing anywhere from four to eight young in a clutch.

Most pairs hatch out their babies in just 18 to 21 days, wean them in four to five weeks, and immediately go back to laying. In the wild state the breeding cycle is controlled by rainfall and the availability of seedling grasses. In captivity the breeding cycle must be interrupted by removing the nest box. This is important to prevent the birds from overproducing. Overproduction can shorten the life of your bird, and the young will become weaker with each clutch.

A hardy budgie, fed a well-rounded diet, should live at least ten years; some may live to fifteen years. Both males and females have similar plumage, but the cere (nostril area) is blue or violet in males and brown or tan in females. Immature females often have a blue shade to the cere, but the under-color will turn to brown or tan when the birds mature at approximately six months of age.

Budgies eat in the morning, roost at midday, and eat again in the late afternoon before returning to the evening roost area. In the wild this roost area is a large tree in which the flock will congregate.

Budgies have an excellent potential for speech if lessons are given regularly and the bird is young. They are chattery birds, responding to music, television, and household sounds, such as running water or the vacuum. Taming the budgie is an easy task if you begin with a young bird, five to ten weeks old. They are inexpensive, available at virtually every retail pet shop, and easy to feed and house.

Opposite: *A pair of beautiful pet quality budgies. Budgerigars are approximately six inches long, and they usually weigh less than one ounce.*

Opposite: A migratory flock of wild budgerigars at a watering hole in Australia. **Right:** A tame budgie perched on the head of the author. **Below:** Other small parrots can be tamed and trained by using the same methods advocated for the budgie in this book.

Although small, the budgie is a hardy little bird that makes a wonderful pet for a mature, responsible child.

Budgies are active, intelligent, playful, and usually very hardy birds. Although they may chatter up a storm, you can easily stop them by placing a cover on the cage for a few minutes and removing it when the birds are quiet. This makes them ideal in the apartment setting.

No other parrot is more highly recommended as a first bird. Budgies can be handled safely by most children—with proper supervision, of course. They are excellent in the elementary school classroom as a class pet. Because daily maintenance is simple, caring for a budgie can be a worthwhile project for even very young children.

A single bird makes the best pet, but two can be kept together comfortably in a standard parakeet cage. Well-supplied pet shops offer a wide variety of parakeet cages and accessories from which to choose. Taming is most easily accomplished with one bird, but if you don't plan to tame the parakeet, get it a companion. You may obtain a second bird and tame it once the original bird is tame. Two birds living together are more interested in their own company and will not readily acquire speech. Obviously, there are many factors to consider before deciding on one budgie or two.

Budgies are the smallest of all Australian parakeets and are often mistakenly called lovebirds. All lovebirds originate in Africa and are a separate and distinct genus incapable of cross-breeding with the Australian shell parakeet.

The best trainer for the young budgie is one with enough time to devote to the task not only for initial taming, but also for the follow through which is required on a daily basis. A tame parakeet will not remain so for long if left to sit in its cage and be ignored. When beginning with a wild parakeet, the trainer must have a cool head and patience.

Both men and women make fine trainers for the budgie. Mature children with calm dispositions can also tame a young budgie. Only one person should attempt to tame the new parakeet. Once tame, the bird should be handled

A pair of crested budgies, a greywing light green and a normal dark green (the bird with the darker marks on the wing). The crest is a relatively new mutation.

Left: *A pet budgie playing in the author's hair. This behavior is not recommended unless the bird has been thoroughly tamed and trained.* **Below:** *This budgie has been trained to come when called.* **Opposite:** *When your budgie has been tamed enough to be permitted to ride on your shoulder, be sure not to forget it is there; it would be quite dangerous to walk outdoors in this situation.*

by all family members that want to befriend it. Above all, the trainer for the new bird must be determined to accomplish the task. A highly motivated trainer can usually tame a five to ten week old budgie in one hour, maybe two.

Do not attempt to tame a budgie if the prospect of being bitten is frightening to you. If the bird should bite you, you may overreact and harm the bird.

Remember, the budgerigar is a very small bird weighing approximately one ounce. You cannot strike a budgie or drop it on the floor and expect it to not get hurt. Very nervous people should not attempt to tame a wild budgie. These small birds tend to flutter around until tamed to sit on your hand and may cause the nervous person undue stress.

A well-tamed budgie can be an excellent companion for a person

Budgies, like most parrots, are chewers; they will gnaw on almost anything. It is imperative, therefore, to be sure the pet budgie is placed in an environment that is free from poisonous plants.

Two budgies kept together will usually get along, but it is a good idea to introduce them before placing them in the same cage.

living alone or one that spends lots of time at home in the daytime.

Budgerigars can live comfortably in both outdoor aviaries and as individuals in a single cage. They are excellent as display birds on patios and in well-

Above: *Visit your pet shop to find the budgie which is best suited to you and your taste.* **Right:** *If possible, you may wish to have the pet shop owner or a veterinarian clip the bird's wing for you.*

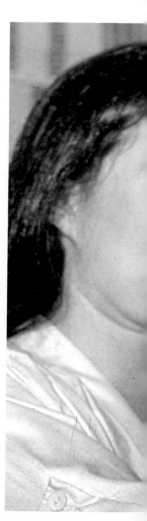

landscaped gardens, and they can live in a classroom setting. No matter what environment the budgie lives in, a few common sense steps must be taken to ensure its good health. Don't place the budgie's cage in a drafty window or doorway. In cold climates, don't place the cage next to a radiator. The kitchen is a poor choice for the bird's cage, for temperatures fluctuate there.

Air-conditioned rooms are fine as long as the bird is not in the path of cold air currents. Cold does not bother the budgie; breezes do.

Indoors as a family pet, the budgie should be kept in the family room where family members spend most of their leisure time. Outdoor aviaries must be complete with a shelter in which the birds can roost and be protected from rain and wind. It is not advisable for the budgie to fly free outside. Larger wild birds such as crows will chase them from the yard.

Shell parakeets are strong flyers, and many have escaped

through open windows and doors. Some of these escapees have adjusted to life in the wild. A large independent flock of shell parakeets is now considered established in central Florida. These birds were introduced to the wild as pet escapees and are now established wildlife in that state.

Below: *If you do not plan to spend a good amount of time with your pet budgie, it may be a good idea to provide it with a companion.* **Opposite:** *The pet budgie requires attention in order to remain happy and interested in life.*

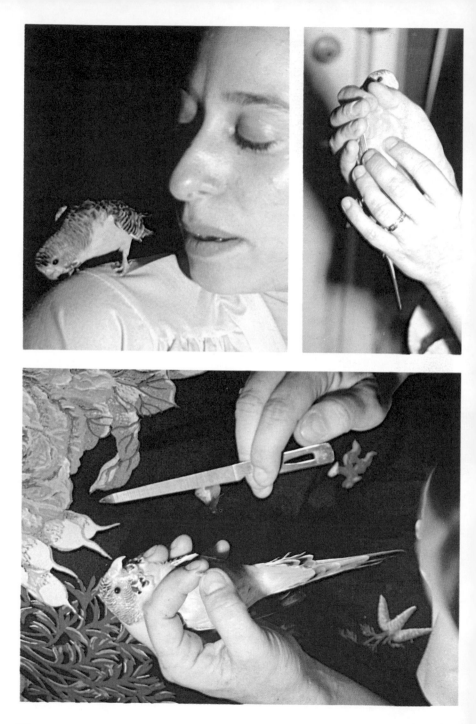

Opposite, top left: *When you find a budgie that interests you, you may wish to ask the pet dealer to let the bird perch on your shoulder if it has been tamed and wing clipped.* **Opposite, top right:** *Feel the bird's breast to be sure that it is not underweight.* **Opposite bottom:** *If necessary, have the budgie's claws filed.* **Above:** *As soon as the bird is taken home, begin to handle it regularly in order to keep it tame.*

Choosing Your Budgie

The retail pet shop is usually the best source for the pet budgie, because these shops usually offer a wide selection of cages and accessories for the pet budgie. Don't buy the bird on impulse. Wait for your pet shop to obtain very young birds. Identify very young budgies by noting the black feather lines that begin just above the cere and stripe the head horizontally from cere to nape. Once these black lines begin to disappear, you can be certain that the bird is ten weeks old or older.

Look around town at the local retailers. Compare price, selection, availability of equipment (supplies and literature), and cleanliness. It is unwise to buy your budgie from a shop where there are dirty cage bottoms or soiled feed receptacles or waterers. If you spot a couple of sick-looking birds with swollen eyes or nasal discharge, it is not advisable to purchase any bird from that cage, no matter how healthy it may appear. You will discover that most retail bird shops keep their budgies in flight cages. When choosing a single bird from a large group in the flight cage, step back to keep from inhibiting the bird's natural behavior.

Spot the youngest birds (those with black stripes from cere to nape) and observe their interactions with others in the cage. Young males are assertive in a group setting and tend to boss others around and chatter in their ears. Young hens are more sedate and may be observed eating from the feed dish, cleaning their feathers or playing by themselves. Birds that sit fluffed up with their heads under their wings or with their eyes closed have a medical problem and should not be purchased.

Watch one bird at a time. Once you have spotted one that suits you, ask the pet shop employee to remove it from the cage for you to examine more closely. Know exactly what you are looking for before you have them remove the bird to avoid holding it longer than necessary. You should feel the bird's breast for good weight. Good weight refers to a normal amount of body mass on either side of the breast bone. Birds that are obviously overweight should alert you to a possible health problem. If the breast bone protrudes, the bird is thinner than it ought to be. Do not purchase a budgie that is thin, for thinness is often a symptom of a serious disorder. Baby budgies should be no thinner than their older siblings if they are in good health.

The healthy budgie is active and alert. The plumage is smooth and even. All feathers should be in place and no bare patches of skin

Opposite: *When choosing your pet budgie, look for a bird that has good weight, clear eyes, and bright plumage.*

Parrots of the World
Joseph M. Forshaw • *illustrated by* William T. Cooper

Left and below: *The small cages sold at department stores are usually inadequate for housing a budgie. The best place to find a proper cage is at your local pet shop.*

visible. The heavy tail and wing feathers should be complete and unbroken. Eyes should be bright and be free of any discharge, tearing or scratches on the eye rings. Birds that hold one eye closed, show swelling around the eye socket, or constantly scratch at their eyes may have a developing eye problem and should not be purchased. Scales or spongy deposits around the eyes or nose indicate the presence of a highly contagious external parasite known as scaly mite. Do not purchase budgies with such deposits.

Nostrils must not be clogged or running. The skin of the cere must be smooth and even in color. Irregularly shaped nostrils may be no problem or they may indicate a genetic irregularity. It is best to purchase a perfect bird, especially since the retail shop offers many from which to choose. Examine the vent for evidence of digestive disorders. The vent must not be soiled. It should be clean and light pink in color.

Check the droppings on the cage bottom. Of course, in a community flight it is impossible to pinpoint an individual's focal remains, but if there is a predominance of bad feces on the

cage bottom, be aware that the bird may be ill. Bad droppings are loose, watery, yellow-orange, light green or all white. Droppings that have no white matter in them may indicate the presence of kidney malfunction (white matter is the urea in bird feces). Healthy droppings are solid in form when wet and contain both dark green and white matter.

Examine the feet, legs and toes. One absent claw is no serious disability for the pet budgie, but many absent claws are undesirable. One missing toe can be compensated for, but two or more missing toes will cause the bird considerable difficulty. Legs and feet should not have sore spots or enlarged scales. Feathers should cover the legs. Grip should

If you plan to keep two budgies, it may be a good idea to purchase both at the same time and from the same cage, as the birds will probably be well acquainted.

be even in both feet, as should temperature. One cold foot and one hot foot may indicate a circulation problem. Weakness in one foot may be a symptomatic malfunction.

The respiration should be slow and even. Birds that have rapid, shallow breathing may have a respiratory illness. You may see a budgie that has heavy breathing in combination with rigid "tail beating." Tail beating refers to a constant up and down motion of the tail (not a flaring of the tail feathers). Tail beating is often symptomatic of both respiratory and digestive ailments.

In review, purchase a budgie with bright eyes, an alert expression, a clean nose and vent, a good amount of body mass on either side of the breast bone, smooth even plumage, and all its toes and claws. The youngest birds will have black stripes from cere to nape and may have black marks on the upper mandible. The youngest are most desirable for taming to talk.

Be sure to check all prospective pet budgies for missing toes.

Opposite: *Use wire cutters to clip the flight feathers on one wing to restrict flight.*
Above and below: *Don't just clip one or two feathers; instead, clip all but the first flight feather (unless any blood feathers are present). Until you have considerable experience, have a professional take care of this procedure.*

Feeding and Maintenance

Budgies are basically seed eaters. In the wild they do not consume hard dry seed. Instead they eat seed in the milk stage, called seedling grasses. In captivity it is imperative that you provide a substitute for seedling grasses. The daily maintenance diet of a single pet budgerigar follows.

A fresh mixture of high quality parakeet mix should be fed daily. A good parakeet mix contains white millet, red millet, canary seed, hulled oats and hemp seed. The millet and canary seed are high in protein and low in calories. The oats and hemp are high in

A nutritious, well-balanced diet will go far in keeping your budgie healthy and happy throughout its life.

calories and provide beneficial oils in the diet. The ratios of the different seeds can be adjusted to suit the needs of your pet. If your budgie is overweight, reduce the amount of oats and hemp in the diet and increase millet and canary seed.

For baby, breeding and convalescing birds, increase the proportion of fattening seed in the diet. In very cold weather, increase the proportion of fattening seed; in very hot weather, decrease it.

Daily, provide a fresh, green, leafy vegetable such as romaine lettuce or chicory, or use fresh branches with leaves such as honeysuckle or cherry hedge. Always wash the branches thoroughly to remove any soil before placing them in the cage. Raw spinach and carrot or turnip tops are fine as long as your pet will eat them. You may want to sprout your own seedling grasses and feed the greens to your budgie. Take a few seeds from the parakeet mix and place them in a shallow dish of soil. Water and leave in indirect sunlight. In about one week you will have grass sprouts; in two weeks you'll have nourishing greens for your bird. If your seed does not grow, it is not good for your bird. In this case, find a better source for your feed. Regular feeding of greens will not cause diarrhea.

Most pet shops sell parakeet seed; the better stores market

Greens are an important part of the diet of budgerigars. Be sure, however, that greens are not given too often; in addition, be sure that all vegetable matter comes from a safe source.

high quality mixes that they put together themselves. By all means buy the fresh mix that your bird shop sells in preference to boxed seed found in the grocery.

Most parakeets do not care for fruit, but yours may be an exception. You may feed it small pieces of apple or orange. Canned corn kernels may be a favorite food or ignored. Experiment with several soft fruits and vegetables to find out if your budgie likes them. If so, provide these on a regular basis to round out the diet.

Every day you must scrub the water dish with hot water, soap and a sponge to remove any residues on the dish. Refill with fresh, cool tap water and add a water-soluble bird vitamin. Do not confuse the water-soluble multivitamin with cold remedies or tonics. Vitamin supplements

As you become more acquainted with your pet (or pets), you will learn its likes, dislikes, and the size of its appetite.

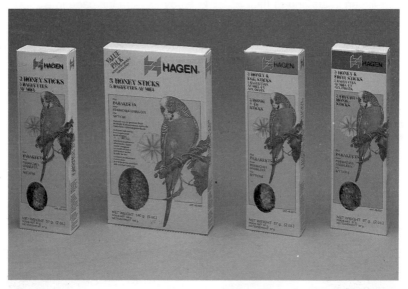

Honey, fruit and egg sticks can be found on display, along with other varieties, at your local pet shop. These flavored seeds can be easily attached to any type of cage and stay fresh for long periods of time. Photo courtesy of Hagen.

should be given every day, not once a week.

Use a few drops of cod liver or wheat germ oil on the parakeet seed every other day. Do not over oil the seed or the bird will refuse to eat it. Salad oil or other types of fat are not recommended. A small amount of the suggested oils in the diet will improve plumage, aid digestion, and prevent skin and scale disorders.

A fresh gravel mixture should be available in a cup, not on the cage bottom. Sand is not recommended for the indoor cage. Mineral grit is an important source of

supplements such as calcium. A high quality gravel mixture contains crushed charcoal. You can usually purchase a high quality grit at the bird shop. Add a bit of iodized table salt to the gravel mix when you change the dish.

There is controversy about the benefit of grit in the diet. Some fanciers believe that if grit is provided on a daily basis, the budgies may become impacted from eating too much. Although this is unlikely, you may want to provide grit for one week every month instead of every day. I have provided grit daily to my birds for over fifteen years and to date none have died as a result of grit impaction. Breeding birds must have grit on a daily basis. A cuttlebone or mineral block, however, must be present in the cage at all times.

Treats for the budgie include millet sprays, fresh branches (leaves and all), egg biscuits and the seed bells sold in your pet shop. Don't overindulge your pet or it will become fat. Fat birds do not have the best chances for a long lifetime. You may give the parakeet fresh boiled egg yolk, but

be very careful to remove any leftovers from the cage in a short time. Spoiled egg can be fatal if ingested by your pet.

Learn to keep a check on your bird's normal daily intake. The budgie that suddenly stops eating or suddenly begins eating double the normal amount may have a developing health problem. If you notice a sudden, dramatic change in your budgie's eating habits, keep watch for any other indications of illness. Weather can affect a bird's appetite, as can molting or egg laying. Be aware that your bird's feeding

Spray millet is especially appreciated by all types of birds. Available from your pet store in a variety of sizes, these nutritious treats make wonderful additions to a well-balanced diet. Photo courtesy of Hagen

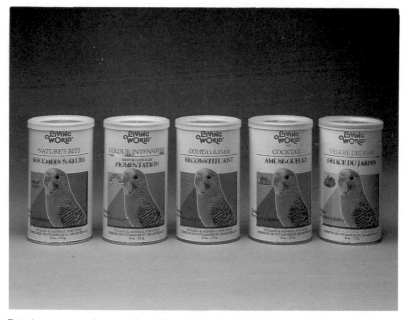

Pet shops carry a large variety of specialized seed mixtures to accommodate the changing needs of your pet. If your bird is molting, breeding, highly active, or just in need of a special treat, there is a mixture that will suit its requirements. Photo courtesy of Living World.

requirements may change according to outside factors; adjust as needed.

At least every other day, clean the cage bottom and change the paper liner. Use newspaper or paper towels. The gravel paper sold by your bird shop can help keep the bird's claws trim, so you should consider using it. Sand is not recommended for the indoor cage as it is messy and may harbor parasites.

Wash the cage and bottom tray periodically with fresh warm water. Dry completely to prevent rusting.

You may wash the perches or scrape them with a perch scraper to remove dirt. If you wash the perches, let them dry completely before replacing them in the cage. Wet perches can cause arthritis and dispose the budgie to other illness.

Wash the water dish every day and the feed dish at least once a week. Dry the seed cup before placing new seed in it.

Most budgies will use a bird bath if one is provided for them. Fill the bird bath with lukewarm water and sit back to see an amusing show. Most budgies take baths readily and will splash around in the dish until most of the water has splashed out. You may use feather shine sprays on the budgie, but if the diet is well balanced you will not need anything to add sheen to the plumage. In warm summer weather the budgie may bathe every day; in winter, limit the bath time. It is best to bathe the bird in the morning to allow ample time for the feathers to dry before sundown. Withhold the bath on rainy days.

Bird bug sprays are best used on the cage and perches. Although they are safe to use on the budgie as directed, you should use your common sense. If kept in clean lodgings, indoor pets rarely harbor feather mites or lice. For these pets, spray the cage before the bird. Outdoor pets are more likely to have external parasites and should be sprayed as directed in the summer months but sparingly in the winter months.

Most Budgies enjoy taking a bath. Pet s⸱⸱, ⸱ carry a number of different designs. This covered bird bath from Hagen is especially nice because it does not allow the water to splash over the entire contents of the cage.

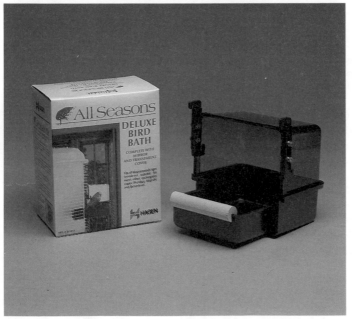

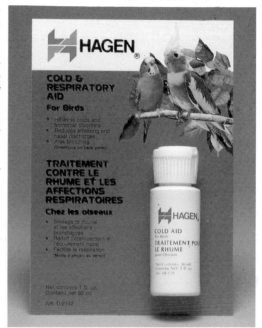

Bathing is good for the budgie. But because budgies have a high metabolism they can deteriorate quickly if they contract respiratory illnesses as a result of being chilled after bathing. Respiratory disease treatments are available at your local pet shop are valuable items to have on hand. Photo courtesy of Hagen.

CLIPPING CLAWS, WINGS, AND BEAKS

The procedures described here are only to be performed by those with experience and training in the area of budgie grooming. Do not attempt them without instruction and practice under the watchful eye of a veterinarian or experienced aviculturist.

The budgie's claws may require an occasional trim. If you keep one wing clipped on your pet, that too must be done routinely. Clipping claws and flight feathers should be done with a small wire clipper. If you keep natural wood branches instead of dowel perches in the bird cage, the claws may never need clipping.

To clip the claws, work in good light and have a styptic powder on hand in case of bleeding. Styptic pencil is too hard to work adequately. Take the small wire cutter or nail clipper and just tip each claw. Only take the tip off the claw no matter how long it is. You can always take more off a badly overgrown claw, but you

Some budgies, especially those that are a breeding pair, will feed each other. A singly-kept budgie may even try to feed its owner.

can't put back anything that has been cut.

If a claw is cut too short and begins to bleed, press a fingertip full of styptic powder against the bleeding spot. Hold for a few seconds and release pressure. Watch the tip for renewed bleeding before going on to the next nail. For heavy continuous bleeding, press the styptic powder into the claw with dry cotton. Hold for at least one minute before

releasing pressure. Replace the budgie in its cage and leave it alone. Don't panic if you notice a drop of blood. If the flow is fast and heavy, you must act quickly to stop it. Most often the bleeding is a slow drip, drip, drip. Wait a few minutes (three to five) to see if the blood clots by itself before catching hold of the bird. Clipping badly overgrown claws down to normal length may take a few trimmings every other week or so.

The flight feathers of one wing may be clipped to restrict the bird's flight. This procedure will help during taming and is a safeguard against losing your pet out the window or door.

Use the small wire cutters and work in good light. Have styptic powder on hand. Leave the outer primary feather on the end of the wing as is. Clip the next ten feathers, leaving at least one inch of feather emerging from the wing. Make certain that you do not cut the feathers off too close to the edge of the wing. Make sure that you can identify any blood feathers that may be present and do not clip them. Blood feathers are new feathers that have not finished growing in. The quill contains a vein that nourishes the feather as it grows. A blood feather may bleed seriously if it is

A lovely opaline olive cock. Opaline budgies have become increasingly popular in recent years.

cut. If you accidentally cut or break a blood feather, use the styptic powder to stop the bleeding.

Remember to clip only one wing. If the job is done properly, the bird's flight will be satisfactorily restricted yet the feathers will grow back properly in the future.

Trim overgrown beaks carefully with a small nail trimmer. Do not trim the tip off of a bird's beak just to dull the bite. You can seriously injure the budgie this way. Trim the beak only to benefit the bird. If the beak is overgrown, the bird will have difficulty cracking seed and eating greens, and it will not be

Natural wood branches make good perches, as one branch will have several different diameters. Be certain, however, that the branch in question has never been sprayed with dangerous chemicals.

It is a good idea to provide several perches with varying widths, as the budgie's feet are exercised as it changes its grip.

able to groom its plumage properly. Be very careful when trimming the beak. You may first try to file off the excess matter. Often the overgrowth is brittle and breaks off easily under the file. If not, use the clippers to take off just a bit at a time until the beak is normally shaped again. File off rough edges. Do not trim the beak if you do not have ample experience. Take the bird to a qualified professional who can

show you the correct procedure. Always have styptic powder on hand in case of accidents. Press a small amount of dry powder into the tip of the beak if it begins to bleed. Place the bird back in its cage and let it settle down. Bleeding should stop quickly if the bird is healthy and the cut is not too deep. Remove the water from the cage overnight and replace it with fresh water in the morning.

Once again, it is very important

Opposite: *An opaline cinnamon grey green pair of budgies, male and female.*
Right: *In addition to exercising the feet, natural wood perches help wear down the budgie's claws.*

that you do not try to clip the claws, wing or beak if you have no experience. Always seek the help of a veterinarian or a professional bird handler and let them show you how to clip. Their method of wing clipping may not be the same as outlined here. You may wish to ask them to follow the suggested clipping method, but watch carefully to see how they do it. Let them show you the difference between blood feathers and feathers that have completely grown in. After you have seen the procedure and practiced sufficiently under proper supervision, you may then want to invest in the necessary equipment and handle the bird's manicures yourself.

HOLDING, CATCHING, AND RELEASING THE BUDGIE

You must learn to catch the bird, hold it properly and release it safely. Budgies are very small birds and they can twist out of your hand before you know it. For this reason it is recommended that you use a small towel or wash cloth to throw over the budgie before you catch it gently but firmly behind the neck.

Use your thumb and first finger to hold the bird around the neck. Keep the towel wrapped around the bird to restrict its vision and to help keep the wings against the torso. Flapping wings can get caught in wire as you try to remove the budgie from its cage. Use the rest of your hand to wrap around the torso. Take the bird out of the cage and use your other hand to turn it over and hold it correctly. Do not try to grab a frightened budgie with your bare hand unless a tenacious bite does not bother you. Budgies grab and hold onto your finger or hand and will refuse to let go. Although superficial, budgie bites can be very painful. You can use a glove to catch the bird, but this is not the preferred method. This may make the bird hand shy. In addition, most people use gloves that are far too big and bulky. It is difficult to feel how hard you are holding the bird in oversized gloves. You may squeeze it very hard or be holding it so lightly that it will fly out of your hand as soon as it gets out of the cage. It is best to use a small towel or bird net.

A trio of brightly colored budgies. When attempting to clip a budgie's nails, etc., be sure all your other birds (and pets) are either in their cages or out of the room.

A pair of budgies will amuse each other, and their owner, with their antics.

If you plan to catch the budgie in a net, have someone help you remove it, get the claws out of the fabric and hold the bird against your towel-covered lap or a padded counter top.

Once you have caught the bird, hold it with your thumb and first finger controlling the head and the rest of your fingers cradling the torso. Place your thumb under the lower mandible if the budgie twists around to bite you. Be careful not to press against the eyes or nostrils. Keep the neck straight and don't pull or push on it. Hold the torso with your other hand, but be certain not to restrict respiration.

Experienced handlers can grab the budgie, manicure or medicate it, and return it to the cage without assistance. The novice should always seek the help of a second person to expedite any procedures. Think about what you are going to do and gather all of the necessary materials before beginning. You do not want to hold the bird any longer than necessary. Always work in good light.

After you have completed the manicure or other procedure, release the budgie with its feet on the floor of the room or place it in the cage, holding it with the feet on the bottom. If you drop the bird onto its cage or let go of it in the air, it may take a dangerous fall. Always release the budgie in an upright position, with the head up and feet down. Let go of the feet first and then the head. Keep the bird's safety in mind at all times.

If you are holding the budgie

Note the curious expressions on these two budgies' faces. Budgerigars have an active interest in things that go on around them.

and someone else is clipping it, do not let go of the bird without fair warning. If it twists a great deal and you are losing your grip, advise your assistant. Your helper can stop what he is doing, help you regain control of the bird and then go back to work.

When you clip the wing, hold it out at the bend. Do not overextend it or you may break it. Don't hold it by the flight feathers on the end of the wing or you may pull them out. When you clip claws, isolate one toe at a time and clip. Go on to the next toe and repeat. Make sure that you do not have a second claw or toe in clipper range before making each cut. Always take off as little as possible; you can always go back and take off more.

Do not begin any clipping procedure without styptic powder on hand. An experienced bird handler can accomplish the entire manicure in approximately five minutes. Work as quickly as possible without taking undue risks of harming the budgie.

These four budgies are a few examples of the many color varieties in which budgerigars come. The plumage color and body type continue to improve as breeders strive for perfection.

Equipment

Just what will you need to begin? A budgie, a cage, parakeet seed and supplements to the diet. Other accessories are not necessary on the first day and can be purchased later. The supplements that you must buy on the first day are a safe soluble vitamin, a good gravel mixture, a mineral block or cuttle bone, and fresh or dehydrated greens.

You may want to get a couple of extra perches to use in taming sessions. A bird stand is not absolutely necessary with a budgie, but it is very handy if you plan to give the bird time out of its cage and do not want it chewing up or messing up your curtains or picture frames. If you have a lot of free time and decide to make your own bird stand out of wood, use ¾-inch plywood for the base and a piece of two by two inch wood for the vertical riser. Drill holes in the riser at various intervals and push ½-inch diameter dowels through for the perches. It would probably be more convenient and more economical to purchase a bird stand at your local pet store. Pet dealers carry a wide variety of pre-assembled stands and would be happy to help you select the best type for you and your bird.

It is wise to buy all of the necessary equipment and accessories at the time that you purchase your budgie. Most pet shops will have a good selection of cages in stock. Buy the largest cage that you can afford. Do not

Below: Budgies are active little birds and enjoy keeping themselves amused. Owners who are away for long periods of time may wish to visit the display of toys at the local pet store. You may have trouble choosing just one! Photo courtesy of Active Bird Toys. *Opposite:* A bird stand is quite convenient if you wish to give your budgie the opportunity to get out of its cage once in awhile.

Bird swings are enjoyed by many budgies and their owners, who like to watch the birds perch and rock back and forth.

try to house the budgie in a finch cage. Since they are very active birds, budgies will make good use of all the cage space that they have, so don't crowd it with too many toys.

Minimum dimensions for a good budgie cage are 16 inches long, 14 inches deep and 18 inches high. Anything smaller is not adequate. Most budgie cages are rectangular, but the round floor model is just as good. The best cages are made entirely of metal.

Plastic tops and bottoms are acceptable, but they do not last as long as metal ones. A wire top is preferable to a closed top. Bottom grills are not necessary in the budgie cage. The cage may be nickelplated or brassplated. Nickel is preferred for durability. Painted metal is not recommended; it chips and is hard to maintain.

Wood or bamboo cages will not hold a budgie. Although small, budgies are active chewers. Bamboo cages are decorative but are not made for budgies.

A friend may offer to give you an old budgie cage that he has in the garage. If the cage is in good condition, take it. Be certain to scrub and disinfect it completely before putting your new pet in it. If you plan to paint the cage bars, be sure to use paint that is labeled "Non-toxic when dry." If these words do not appear on the label, do not use the paint. Do not let the hardware store tell you that it is safe; be certain that "Non-toxic when dry" is clearly printed on the paint can.

It is usually best to buy a new cage for your budgie rather than trying to recondition an old one. The cage can be plain or ornamental as long as the bird is comfortable in it.

The cage door must close securely or your inquisitive pet will

When preparing to train a pet budgie, be certain that all other birds, pets, and people are out of the room.

surely learn to pop it open. Perches must be made of wood, not plastic. Dowels should be ½-inch in diameter; if possible, use natural wood, which has a variety of grips. The claws will stay trimmed if the budgie sits on natural wood. The sandpaper perch covers that your pet shop carries are meant to keep the claws trimmed, but natural wood is preferred. The budgie can occupy itself all day chewing on the bark of its perch. Only use branches that you know have not been sprayed or treated with chemicals. Most cages come with two or three dowel perches and a swing. You can rearrange these to provide your pet with maximum living space.

Feeders are usually made of hard plastic. Your pet shop probably sells replacement cups

Since it is a fact that most budgies will chew upon their cages, it is imperative that the bars are made of safe material and are covered with non-toxic paint.

It cannot be overstated that all budgie owners must be sure that any branches or plants placed in the cage have never been treated with dangerous chemicals.

for the cages that they carry. Replace the cups in reconditioned cages. You may build your own cage and use feeders and waterers made of ceramic material, plexi-glass, plastic and stainless steel. The water cup must be cleaned thoroughly with hot water and soap every day. This is perhaps the best

preventative method for protecting your budgie's health. Feed dishes can be cleaned less often but at least once weekly.

You may be interested in buying a bird net. These can be very handy when your bird must be caught in a hurry or is an untamed escapee. Gloves are not recommended for taming a young budgie but may be helpful for the novice trainer if trying to tame an older bird. Buy tight-fitting gloves or cotton gloves at the sporting goods store.

Toys can be homemade or store bought. Either way, be sure that they are not going to fall apart into pieces that your budgie may swallow and choke on. It is dangerous to hang toys from the top of the cage if the bird can get twisted in them. Always use your common sense when choosing toys for the budgie.

Soft wood chew toys are excellent, as are small bells with secure clappers. Ladders are ignored by some budgies and adored by others. Mirrors should not be placed in the bird's cage during initial taming, as they can in some instances interfere with the budgie acquiring speech.

Left: *A pair of budgies enjoying each other's company.* **Opposite:** *Two characteristics of the budgie's plumage are the black bars and throat spots.*

Taming and Training

Before you begin to tame the newly acquired budgie, prepare an adequate taming area in which to work. A small room such as the bathroom or a small bedroom is recommended. It is imperative that you cover any hard floors with padding and remove sharp objects that the budgie may bump into as he flaps around in the beginning sessions. Cover mirrors to prevent the bird from flying into them.

When working in a room filled with furniture, you will find yourself chasing the untame bird out from under the furniture more than actually handling it. Therefore, an uncluttered room is recommended. Always use the same area for the initial sessions, and, once the bird is hand tamed, begin introducing it to the other rooms in the house.

Only one person should attempt to tame the new pet bird. This person should work alone to avoid confusion, which will stress the bird unnecessarily. Basic taming should begin as soon as you get the budgie home. You have

Left: *A lutino budgie.*
Opposite: *Budgies are intelligent birds that can be taught a number of tricks. Many budgies will learn to climb a ladder on their own.*

probably transported the bird home from the pet shop in a small cardboard carrier, so take this into the prepared taming area, place the box down on the floor and open it up. It is best to allow the budgie to come out of the box on its own; this usually takes a very short time.

Once the bird is out on the padded floor, it will usually attempt to fly. The bird clipped as recommended will not fly well; it will tire fairly soon and begin to turn its attention to you. You should have two short dowels; regular cage perches will work as well. Use the dowels to teach the bird to step up onto the stick when it is offered. With very young birds, this is usually not necessary because they hand tame easily

without attempting to bite. With older or nervous birds, the perch training is recommended to teach the budgie the basic behavior of stepping up when presented with an adequate perch. Once the bird automatically steps up onto an offered perch, substitute your hand and see how easily it will step up. If this is not the case, do more work with the perch, drilling the budgie to step up and off until the behavior is ingrained. Now return to the drill with your hand. Most budgies learn to sit on your hand in less than one hour if they are trained in a prepared taming area devoid of outside confusion.

Once you have the budgie stepping onto your hand from the floor and from the perch, drill it in stepping from one hand to the

Toy swings take advantage of the budgie's desire to perch, and bells take advantage of their natural curiosity.

A budgie will usually climb to the highest perch it can find in a given area. This is why one often sees budgies seated upon their owners' shoulders or heads

other. Do this slowly and steadily to give the budgie confidence in you as a secure perch. Let the bird step onto your shoulder, but tie back your hair and remove earrings to prevent it from getting tangled up. A newly acquired bird may become frightened and give you a good bite if it gets tangled. Shoulder training comes a bit later in taming and should be decided upon by you, the trainer, not by the bird. Remember, however,

that it is a natural tendency for birds to seek the highest available perch, for it represents security to them.

In the first few lessons, stay low to the floor to protect your budgie from taking a bad fall. Undoubtedly the budgie will jump from your hand a few times, so don't lift it high off the floor until it is fairly steady on your hand.

Never grab the bird if it tries to escape from you. In a small room it can't go far. Let it go and begin again. Grabbing the bird to prevent it from escaping does not work; it only frightens the bird and gets you bitten. You may even come out of a grab with a handful of tail feathers but no bird.

Move slowly with the budgie on your hand and pull it close to your body for security. If you hold it out in front of you and try to walk with it, you are inviting it to jump. Move slowly around the taming area before attempting to move to another room. Use your judgment as to when your budgie is ready to move to a strange room. Spend a

very short time there and return to the taming area. As training progresses, spend more time in different rooms with the budgie until it remains with you no matter where you go in the house. Do not go out into the yard with your new budgie. It would be far too traumatic and may turn into a tragedy.

Offer your budgie a small piece of millet spray during the taming lessons. Millet spray is a favorite food for most of the budgies I have known and can be a very effective training aid.

Always move slowly and speak

Once your budgie has been tamed, it will come to enjoy the attention it receives from its owner during training sessions.

A normal grey cock budgie. Gray coloration is showing up in many budgerigar varieties, e.g. greywings.

to the new bird in a soft voice to calm it. Always offer your hand to the bird and coax it to step up by gently pushing against its legs. Never pick up the bird from behind until your relationship with it develops that type of intimacy. If necessary, cup your hands, with fingers laced together, to get the budgie to step up. Eventually you will be able to switch to having it step onto your finger or the back of your hand.

Taming a young budgie is one of the easiest tasks in bird taming that you are likely to encounter. Stay calm, be determined and give your bird frequent lessons.

It is wise to keep an untamed bird in a separate room from other birds, as the wild budgie will be more interested in those other birds than in its lessons.

Repetition is the key to successfully taming a newly bought bird of any kind.

Although the first lesson may take up to one hour, it is not necessary to always devote an hour's time to training your bird. It is far better to give three or four ten-minute lessons in one day than to wait for the day that you have an hour to spend on taming the bird. Taming must be practiced every day for the bird to reach its full potential as a tame pet.

Once the budgie is tame to one member of the household, it is advisable to have other family members handle the bird and attempt to make friends with it if the bird is meant to be a family pet. Young children should always be supervised when handling any small or large birds for their mutual safety.

Once you have finished the

lesson, you can place the bird back in its cage or on a prepared bird stand. Never leave the budgie unsupervised in the house. They have a way of getting into mischief just as children do. You may spend frantic minutes trying to locate the budgie only to find it cuddled up in the fold of your draperies or in a bookcase. Some budgies are so bold that they will walk on the floor and meet their demise because you stepped on them without realizing that they were there. Remember that you are responsible for the bird's safety in your home and act wisely.

Try to bring the bird home from the pet shop in the morning; this allows ample time for you to begin taming it before putting it to sleep in a strange place. Don't transport the bird in the rain or snow. If you see a particular bird that you want, have the pet shop put it aside for you until the weather is better. You will probably be purchasing a cage from the shop at the time that you purchase the budgie. It is best, however, to transport the bird home in the small cardboard box that your pet shop will provide. This will protect it from drafts and undue stress from traffic and other city noises that

A pair of budgies playing on a seesaw ladder. Remember to completely tame and train one budgie at a time before attempting to train two birds together.

will usually upset the bird.

Never use food deprivation as a taming method with a newly acquired budgie. Not only does this undermine the bird's health, but it is unnecessary. If you put the time into taming the bird and are consistent with your lessons, you will be rewarded with a very tame pet. Do not work with the budgie in total darkness. This is a popular method, but it seems to me that neither the bird nor the trainer can see well enough to merit working in a dark room. Don't wet the bird. This is another old wives' tale concerning a good taming method. Wetting the bird subjects it to undue stress in an already stressful situation and can cause it to become ill. One fact is clear: it is better to have a healthy untame bird than a sick tame one. You cannot possibly tame a sick bird.

Keep in mind that parrots do not have sweat glands and their excess body heat is expelled

Always be patient and consistent when taming and training your pet or pets. Several short sessions usually work better than one or two long ones.

When you notice that your budgie is becoming distracted or overly excited, give the bird time to rest.

through the respiratory system in the form of panting. If your bird begins to pant uncontrollably, allow it time to rest before beginning to tame it again.

DAILY ROUTINE

A good daily routine is as follows:

1) Feed and clean the bird cage, wash the water cup and refill with fresh water with vitamins added.

2) Change the cage bottom.

3) Give daily lessons on taming and advanced training.

4) Keep the bird out of drafts and do not subject it to undue stress.

5) Place the bird in its cage and cover it in cold weather; covering the cage is not necessary in warm weather.

DESTRUCTIVE BEHAVIOR

Many budgie owners allow their pets the freedom of the house as flighted birds. This often leads to the bird chewing up picture frames, curtains, furniture and other articles of value. There is virtually no way to eliminate

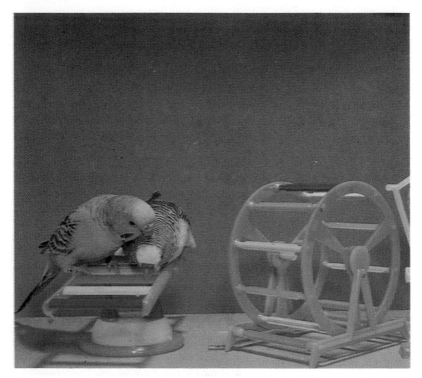

If a budgie is given a companion or adequate attention from its owner, it should not have any reason to develop the bad habits that are brought on by boredom.

chewing activity in any members of the parrot family, but this behavior can be channeled. Give the bird plenty of fresh branches or soft pieces of wood to chew.

Biting is an undesirable behavior and must be dealt with rationally. Do not strike a budgie for biting you. This does not help to eliminate the behavior and can in fact increase the incidence of biting.

Chattering can become a problem if the budgie continues without a let up. In this case, it is very effective to cover the cage for no more than five to ten minutes. Once the bird is quiet, uncover its cage and reinforce the good behavior with a reward of millet spray or by handling the bird out of its cage. Again, be aware before you purchase a budgie that a happy bird is a chattery one. This is normal behavior and must be part of your lifestyle if you plan to live with a parrot of any kind. Running water, vacuum cleaners, music and other household noises always inspire the budgie to chatter. If you cannot live with a happy chattering bird, give it to someone who will appreciate it or don't get one in the first place. Better yet, teach a chattery budgie to talk; he will usually replace his chattering noises with speech and become a source of pride and entertainment for the owner.

One other behavior problem is worth mentioning here—jealousy. Jealousy may be directed at other family members, if a budgie feels that its relationship with the favored person is threatened, or toward a second bird that you decide to buy to keep the original one company. Whenever you introduce a new bird into the budgie's cage, you must watch carefully for any signs of aggression toward the new bird. If

Be aware that an established budgie may become jealous of any people, bird, or other pets. In order to prevent this, it is important to introduce the pet budgie to other members of the household.

necessary, introduce the new bird to the older bird in a new cage. In really extreme cases you may have to keep the birds in separate cages side by side for a few weeks before placing them together. Even if the older bird is not actively nasty toward the new one as you sit and watch, he may be when you are absent. Check the weight of the newly bought budgie to be certain that the older bird is not keeping it from eating an adequate amount of feed.

Don't be unduly alarmed when acquiring a new budgie; the old bird may accept the new one readily and befriend it immediately. This is just a caution to keep an eye on the relationship between an older established bird and a newly acquired younger bird to prevent unnecessary loss and heartache.

Escape artists must be dealt with by placing a heavy catch on the cage door; otherwise the bird will be leaving and returning to its

When first introducing a new budgie to one that you already have, be sure to keep an eye on it for awhile. Check the new bird's weight, and keep an eye out for any injuries.

A recessive pied grey green cock. Male budgerigars are usually more aggressive than females.

cage at will. If this agrees with your lifestyle, there is no problem. If you are a working person, it is best to know that the budgie is secure in its cage while you are not at home.

To catch an escaped budgie, you should use a net. If you do not have a net, use a large towel to throw over the bird and catch it;

keep it wrapped in the towel and return it to its cage until you can get it clipped, if you so desire.

If your budgie should get out the door or window and fly off into a tree, place its cage in clear view of the bird with food and water in the regular cups. Take a whole strand of millet spray and place it just inside the cage. Try to lure the bird down, but don't scare it off by attempting to climb the tree and grab it. If possible, get another budgie from a friend and place that bird in its cage in clear view of the escaped bird. It may take three to five days before the escaped bird elects to fly down to its cage. If it does fly down, do not frighten it off by running up to it to close it in. Most likely the bird will be hungry and thirsty enough to remain in its cage when you approach slowly to close the door and bring it back indoors.

Untamable budgies are very rarely encountered if bought from a reliable pet shop. If you buy an old bird or find that the budgie you have purchased is still frantic after many hours of devoted work in attempting to tame it, perhaps you can trade it back to the pet dealer for another bird. Be realistic, however. If you have only given the bird sporadic taming lessons, a new bird will become no more tame than the one that you

If your budgie should escape outdoors, the worst thing you can do is chase after it, as this will frighten an already nervous bird. Instead, leave its cage and a dish of food where the budgie can see it, and wait patiently for the bird to come home.

Headstudy of an opaline cinnamon skyblue cock budgerigar.

already have. If you do not have time to tame the budgie, it is best not to attempt it. Allow the bird to live comfortably in a large enough cage to allow it free flight. Remember that budgies are probably the most easily tamed of all parrot type birds and if you fail with more than one or two, the problem is not with the bird but with your approach to taming it.

Like many of their larger counterparts, budgies can develop a strong attachment to one person and harbor jealous feelings toward all other people and birds. To avoid this situation, have different family members become involved in the daily maintenance of the cage: feeding, watering and handling. The jealous budgie is far easier to control in a family setting than an Amazon or macaw; this makes the budgie a far better choice for a family pet.

Left: *The budgerigar has a good capacity for speech as well as for learning tricks.* **Opposite:** *When attempting to speech train a budgerigar, be sure that it is kept away from all other birds, as their chatter will distract the budgie and will make it forget what it has learned.*

The sex of the budgie is not important in its potential for tamability, but if you plan to teach your bird to speak, it is best to obtain a young male bird. Although the female may acquire speech (and I have personally known some female budgies that spoke), the male is a more reliable student.

Speech training differs greatly from basic taming. The basic characteristics of a tame bird are considered to be the following: the bird will step onto your hand readily when it is presented in a confident manner; the bird will not bite unless provoked (i.e., grabbing and restraining the bird);

the bird will be retrievable from any place in the house; and it will step into and out of the cage when you desire.

Trained budgies are considered to have more sophisticated and variable behaviors. The trained bird has learned that certain behaviors, when performed on command, will get it attention. Speech training is an advanced form of training, and although an untame bird will learn to speak, the tame budgie is more likely to speak on command than the untame bird. Command speech refers to the budgie repeating you immediately upon request. Many budgies acquire large

vocabularies but do not talk on command and instead speak when they choose to do so; as soon as you try to make the bird speak to a friend or even to you, it acts like a clam!!!

To teach the budgie to speak it is recommended that your lessons are kept short, repetition is frequent each day, and concentration is placed on the same material until the bird has mastered it. If you attempt to teach the bird to say one thing, get tired of repeating it and decide to work on something else, you will confuse the bird and probably

never get it to speak audibly.

Work on only one or two syllable words to begin. "Hi" and "Hello" are good words. Say the word slowly and distinctly and follow with the bird's name. For example, if your bird's name is Groucho, say "Hello, Groucho" whenever you give it a lesson.

Don't expect to hear the word perfectly the first time that your bird tries to repeat it. Most birds practice for a long time before they say the word to you, so listen for the first attempt to duplicate your sound and reward the bird. As lessons continue, the bird

Food rewarding is a good method of reinforcement for the budgie that is being speech trained.

As the voices of women and children are closer in sound to the high-pitched chatter of budgerigars, the birds will have an easier time duplicating these sounds.

should begin to duplicate your sounds with more accuracy and you should demand more from the budgie in later lessons. Budgies are naturally vociferous, and the best times of day for speech lessons are in the morning and late afternoon as the sun is setting. The bird will chatter when you speak to it. Reward it for every attempt to verbalize whether it sounds like a bird sound or not. Next, work for a two-syllable verbalization. If you have gotten the bird to repeat "How are you," work for the bird to reply with a three-syllable sound and work closer and closer to the desired sound. Begin to delay giving a reward once the bird has demonstrated that it can work closer and closer to the desired goal, exact duplication of sound. Do not, however, make the mistake of withholding reward completely even if the bird does not seem to be in tune to the lesson. Always try to end the lesson on a high point instead of a low point. That way the bird will become more consistently responsive as the lessons

A recessive pied mauve budgerigar. This particular variety of budgie is rather difficult to breed.

progress.

Always be realistic when attempting to teach a budgie to speak. Although some have been able to develop extensive verbal and musical repertoires, the majority will acquire a few simple sounds in a high-pitched voice. By no means can a budgie's voice quality and speech potential be compared to their larger Amazon relatives.

You can conduct the lesson with the bird inside its cage, on a stand, or sitting on your hand. There is no need to cover the bird cage or darken the room. Try to work without extraneous noises that will distract the bird and the trainer. Leave the T.V. off and don't let your stereo blast when you are giving serious speech lessons.

A woman's or child's voice is

most easily duplicated by a small bird. No matter who the speech trainer is, that one person must be consistent in giving the lesson every day. Working for five to ten minutes at a time four to five times a day seems to work better than one 30 to 40 minute lesson once a day. Keep in mind that some budgies may respond better to the long lesson, but I have found the short frequent lessons to be more effective.

Only one person should work on teaching the budgie its first words. Once the bird begins to repeat with accuracy, the other family members should become involved in the drill process if they desire.

I prefer the live lesson to the endless tape-recorded one. Recorded lessons are fine to

Just as in taming, you should keep the room in which you speech train your budgie free from the distractions of other birds, pets, or noises.

Above: *A trio of beautiful blue-series budgies.* **Opposite:** *After the budgie has mastered several words, other people may begin to help in its speech training.*

supplement your live lessons, but remember that you are teaching the bird to speak in a certain environment and if that environment is with no people present, the bird will probably speak only with no people there. Some of these budgies will talk up a storm when you are out of sight in another room but will remain silent when you are in the room.

To review: work from the simple one and two-syllable words to the more difficult phrases. Work in the morning and late afternoon or whenever you find that your bird is most naturally chattery. Keep the background noise to a minimum. Give lessons daily, keep them short, and give them as often as possible each day. Teach one thing at a time and make sure that your bird has mastered it before going on to new words.

Training for Tricks

ADVANCED CONDITIONED RESPONSE

Budgies, although small, are some of the most talented trick-trainable birds with which I have ever worked. They can learn to perform a number of amusing tricks if training is given regularly in a prepared training area and the trainer is motivated to have the bird succeed.

For trick training it is best to begin with a young bird, but tamed older birds can also be trained successfully. The key to success is to follow through on what you begin. If you begin a certain lesson and change your approach as you go along, or skip giving lessons because your other activities are more important, it is better not to begin trick training. Otherwise you may train the bird that the status quo is acceptable and he will have a difficult time understanding that you are working for perfection. If you simply don't have the time to follow through, don't begin trick training. For young children with good self-confidence, trick training a budgie can be a rewarding experience for both bird and child. My first trick trained birds were budgies that hatched out in my first attempt at bird keeping. At

Left: *Budgies can be taught to perform a number of amusing tricks if they are properly trained.* **Opposite:** *Be sure that you do not overwork your birds, as stress can lead to illness in budgies.*

that time I was in elementary school.

As with speech training, you must be realistic when you decide on a trick to teach your budgie. It can be taught to pull little wagons or to place tokens in a container. You can try teaching it to display its wings upon command or bob its head to music. Teach the bird to lie on its back in your hand or fly to your hand when you call it by name (of course the bird will have to be flighted to do this).

These are just a few of the simpler tricks that your budgie can learn with consistent, determined training. Keep the first lessons very short and reward the bird even though it may not seem at all interested in what you are doing. Try to end your lessons before the bird gets fidgety. Do not extend the lesson for more than fifteen minutes even though it has mastered the desired behavior.

Reward your bird just for attending to you at first. Later increase your demands by withholding reward until the bird attempts to perform correctly for you. Millet spray is excellent for rewarding the bird. Only give a tiny amount so that the bird will swallow it quickly and be ready to repeat the desired behavior. Always reward the bird immediately when it performs

A pair of budgies in an exhibition cage. Some bird clubs hold exhibitions of trained budgies.

If you plan to train two birds for a particular trick, be sure that they are compatible.

correctly. Don't expect too much too fast, but some of these clever little parrots will amaze you at how quickly they can acquire new behavior.

A few other simple tricks for the budgie are climbing ladders and ringing a bell at the top, tightrope walking, and hopping on command. Watch the budgie to see what its natural behaviors are.

Try to reinforce these until they become conditioned responses. In this way you can develop your own unique repertoire of tricks.

Only teach one trick at a time. Keep lessons short. Only one trainer should begin teaching the bird a trick. Once a trick is mastered, different family members can drill the bird, but all should follow the same basic approach and reward in the same way. Do not expect your budgie to become a bicycle rider or roller skater unless you are able to manufacture the props by yourself.

TAKING THE BIRD OUTSIDE

Taking the bird outside with you is not recommended unless you follow a strict regimen of training before attempting this. You must clip the bird's wing to begin this training. Teach it to remain on a stand or on your shoulder and work on this indoors for some time before attempting to take the bird outside.

Unless you have a quiet backyard or a protected area, it is best not to try taking the bird out. Remember that neighborhood

Budgies can be taught to perform many types of tricks. The key to success is to work with their natural behavior and to teach complex tricks one step at a time.

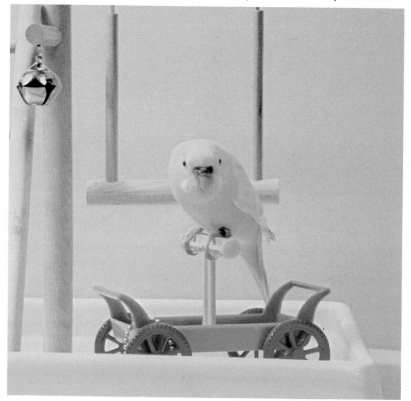

A yellowfaced grey cock budgerigar. When training your pet budgie, remember to keep the bird's safety in mind at all times.

dogs and cats, not to mention traffic noises, sirens and large wild birds, can frighten your budgie into flying off even on its limited wing power. If you are in a quiet neighborhood and can follow through on teaching the bird to remain on a stand outside, never, never leave it unattended. Even one or two minutes of inattention can be the cause of an accident to your budgie.

First Aid and Illness

When you first buy your budgie, it is best to get the name of a competent veterinarian that treats birds often, not just once in a while. Ask your retailer the name of the vet that he uses or, better yet, ask a friend that has owned birds in the past and has had good luck with a particular vet. A vet that has parrots of his own is usually more interested in learning to deal with avian diseases than one that owns horses.

The study of avian medicine is a fairly new endeavor for all of the people involved in the bird industry. This is because in the past birds were imported readily in large numbers and were far less expensive than they are today. Due to the complicated restrictions on importing birds, the prices at

Below: *Before introducing a new budgie to an established one, be sure that both birds are in excellent health.* **Opposite:** *Healthy budgerigars have bright, clean plumage and clear eyes.*

If you suspect that a particular bird is ill, remove it immediately from all your other birds, place it in quarantine, and clean the cage in which it was kept. In addition, keep an eye on the other birds in that cage.

both wholesale and retail levels have increased tremendously. Although the majority of budgies found in retail shops are domestically bred, budgie owners have benefitted from the new interest in avian medicine.

The inexperienced bird owner usually does not notice that his pet is ill until the bird has reached a critical stage. Once the budgie sits fluffed up, refuses to eat and sleeps most of the day, it is very

difficult to successfully treat whatever illness it has.

For this reason, it is imperative that the budgie owner know what normal healthy behavior is for his pet. It is wise to keep a daily check on the droppings when you clean out the cage. Don't just throw the paper out; look at it. If the droppings deviate from the norm (not just one or two loose stools but a whole day's worth), begin looking for other symptoms of illness. Normal stools contain both dark green and white matter and have solid form. Yellow, orange, light green, all white or very watery droppings are often an indication of illness.

It is unwise to attempt to diagnose and treat your budgie without the advice of a good vet. Although your retail pet shop may offer nonprescription drugs for a variety of illnesses, it is far better to seek the vet. Call and make an appointment before you bring the bird to his office. In the meantime you should keep the sick bird very warm and quiet. A temperature of 90 to 95 degrees F is not too warm for a bird whose normal body temperature is 105 to 108 degrees F.

Transport the bird to the vet in a closed carrier or a small box to protect it from temperature

A dominant Dutch pied olive green budgie. The ideal budgie would have a tail that is carried a little higher.

fluctuation and stress. Take a sample (from that morning) of stool to the vet for a parasite check if the bird eats a great deal and still loses weight.

Discharge from the eyes or nose or swelling around the periphery of the eyes must be considered symptoms of serious malady. See the vet immediately. Soiled or distended vents can also indicate illness. Labored or irregular breathing can be symptomatic of many disorders and must be treated by the vet.

Lumps and bumps on the bird's body may be benign or terminal. Many budgies develop fat tumors due to a lack of exercise and an overrich diet. Do not assume that your budgie has cancer if it develops a lump on the body. Often these lumps are easily removed and do not seriously affect the longevity of the bird if treated promptly.

Accidents are another matter. If your bird flies into a window or mirror head first and falls to the floor without moving or begins to make a moaning sound, it may be in shock. Shock is often the immediate cause of death with budgies, so learn to recognize the symptoms and take action. You do not have time to take the bird to

Headstudy of a lovely violet budgie. A healthy budgie must always have good weight.

A healthy cage or aviary environment for budgerigars will allow plenty of room for all birds housed there. Budgies need exercise to prevent them from becoming obese. Obesity in budgies is a dangerous health hazard.

Prevention is probably the best method for keeping your budgie healthy and safe from accident.

the vet until you have administered first aid.

The symptoms of shock may be pupils that do not react to light, shallow breathing, moaning sounds or no reaction to your touch. Any budgie that has suffered a traumatic injury and lies still while exhibiting these symptoms should be treated for shock.

Treat shock by moving the bird as little as possible. Wrap it in a soft towel (a wash or hand cloth is large enough for a budgie), place the bird in a warm box or other container, and stabilize the temperature at 90 degrees F. Dim the lights and do not try to feed the bird seed or give it water. By so doing you could kill the bird. Be certain not to overheat the budgie. Place it gently into a small box wrapped in a soft cloth and place the box on top of a heating pad. Never use a radiator or gas heater to warm a bird. Carefully watch the heat with an accurate thermometer. The thermometer should be one of the essential supplies that you have on hand in case of emergency. Place the thermometer inside the box beneath the budgie. Use newspaper or a towel between the heating pad and the box to get the heat where you want it.

Look in on the bird occasionally to see whether it has recovered. Some come out of shock quickly and usually make a quick recovery. Others may remain in

A lovely yellow budgerigar. Budgerigars of different color varieties sometimes have different body types.

shock for long periods of time. In either case, consult your vet for follow-up care.

Budgies may fall prey to cats or dogs and be injured seriously or superficially. If the budgie has an open bleeding wound, use clean cotton swabs dipped in hydrogen peroxide with the excess liquid pressed out. Press the swab gently against the bleeding wound and hold it there for a minute or two to see if the bleeding stops. When the bleeding stops, sprinkle the wound with antiseptic powder.

When bleeding is really severe, it may take plain pressure with a clean cotton swab to stop the flow.

A budgerigar with scaly face. This condition is caused by a mite infestation and should be treated immediately.

A normal cinnamon greywing. Note the brownish markings on the wing.

By all means stop any bleeding first; even when a budgie is in shock, stop all the bleeding before you treat it for shock.

Broken wings, legs or toes may or may not be emergencies, depending upon the type of break. Fractures, breaks which do not push the bone through the skin, are not emergencies. Keep the bird warm and quiet until you get to the vet. When a bone has emerged through the skin, you must seek emergency aid. Most vets have an answering service that can refer you to an emergency aid station at any hour. In any case, you must not excite the bird. Keep it warm and quiet until you can get aid.

Budgies may get twisted in loose threads from their cage covers or in toys that you thought were safe. Approach the bird slowly to avoid frightening it. Speak reassuringly to the bird as

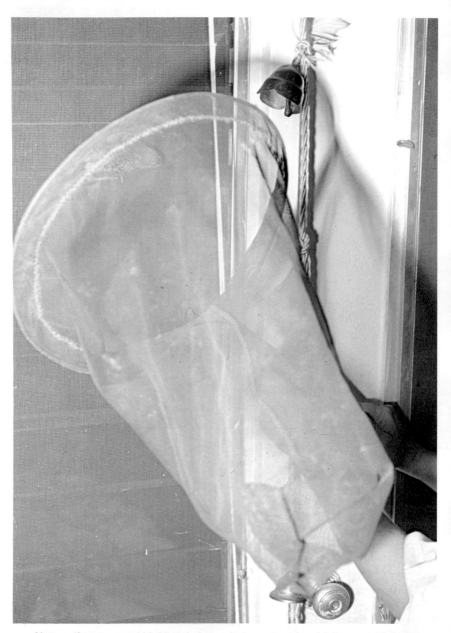

Above: *If an escaped bird heads for a window, you may wish to use a bird net to capture it.* **Opposite top:** *Place your hand over the net to gently pin the bird down.* **Opposite bottom:** *Use your other hand to remove it from the net, making sure that its claws are not caught in the netting.*

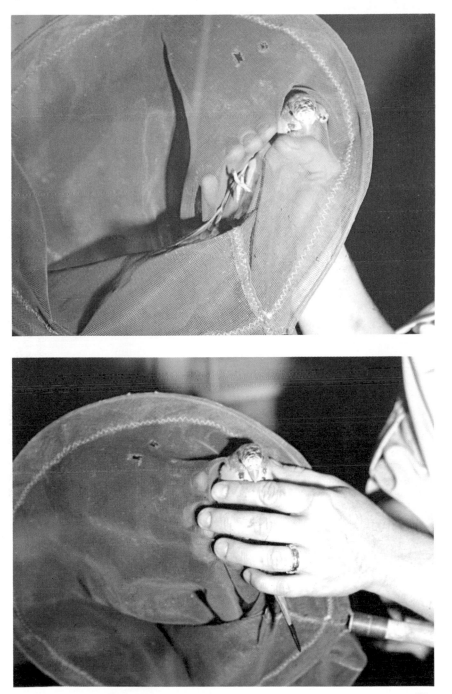

A white cock budgerigar. If there is any doubt as to the health of your budgie, take it to the veterinarian.

you untangle it. If you truly want to keep it from further harm, try to ignore the fact that the bird may bite you in fear. Once untangled, the limb should be carefully examined. If the limb is swollen but otherwise undamaged, place the bird back in its cage. Cover the cage halfway and keep an eye on the bird. Do not grab it

unnecessarily. You may have to call the vet if swelling does not abate or if contusions are apparent.

Chipped beaks, cracked nails or broken blood feathers may bleed and clot by themselves or bleed severely. Use styptic powder and press it into the bleeding spot with clean cotton. Hold for a minute or two until bleeding stops. Place the bird in its cage and keep it quiet.

There are so many possible maladies that may affect your pet and accidents that might happen that it is far better to use preventative measures than to treat these conditions once they occur. Use common sense, keep your bird cage and feed cups clean, use a good quality feed, and use the suggested supplements. Always monitor your pet's activity when it is at liberty in the house to avoid accidents.

The most common cause of death for captive budgies is the common cold. Respiratory and digestive disorders can be cured if caught and treated properly and promptly. If ignored or unnoticed, they are often fatal.

Keep your budgie clean and consult a qualified vet whenever

When you keep more than one budgie in the same cage, be sure that there are enough perches for all the birds.

Above: *If your pet budgie is not tame, you may have problems in removing it from the cage.* **Opposite:** *Learn the proper way to grip and hold the budgie.*

you feel it is necessary.

Feather problems can result from nutritional deficiencies, genetic disorders or nervous tension. If your budgie begins chewing feathers, check the diet and adjust if necessary. Supply the bird with fresh branches to guide its natural tendency to chew.

If you suspect external parasites, spray the cage with a commercially prepared preparation, not a homemade concoction. Remove all feed and water dishes when you clean, disinfect and spray the cage. Spray the perches and allow them to dry before placing the budgie back in its cage. Spray the bird lightly if you really think it necessary, but do not overuse bird bug sprays.

Swollen sore feet, lameness,

Budgies can adapt to some temperature variation, but it is best to keep them in a room where the temperature is constant. In addition, be sure to keep them out of drafts.

A grey green hen budgerigar. Egg binding in hens is a serious problem which is best left for a veterinarian to handle.

and developmental paralysis should be diagnosed by the vet and treated according to his recommendations.

Egg binding may result in a female budgie even in the absence of a mate of the opposite sex. Birds go into breeding condition as a response to the environment. Seek advice from the vet if you suspect egg binding. Keep the bird warm and humidified but not wet. Do not try to push the egg out of the bird; let the vet perform all procedures of this nature. Egg binding can result from a lack of exercise, nutritional deficiencies, or genetic dispositions.

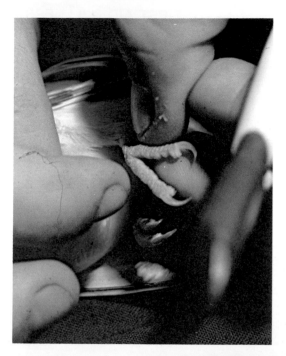

Left: *Be careful not to cut the budgie's claw too close to the vein. If the claw starts to bleed, however, use styptic powder to stop the bleeding.* **Below:** *Be sure to remove all loose threads from the budgie's cage cover, or the bird may become tangled in them.*

Right: *When cutting the budgie's claws, isolate the individual claw before you cut.* **Below:** *After cutting the claw, file it down so there are no rough edges.*

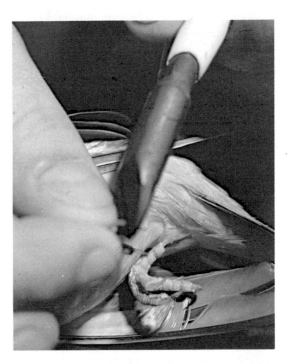

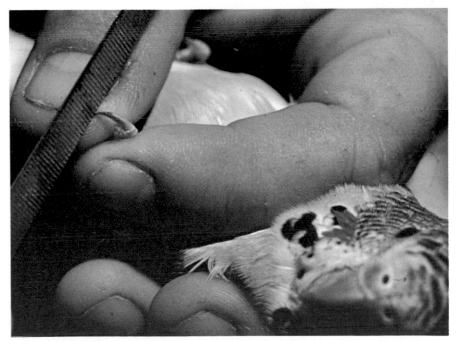

Breeding Budgies as a Hobby

Budgies are prolific breeders and make an excellent choice for the beginning hobbyist. I was first successful at breeding budgies when I was ten years old. This may sound unrealistic, but because the budgerigar is such a free breeder with such simple requirements as to space and diet enrichment, there is very little that the budgie owner needs to do to accomplish a successful breeding experiment.

Begin the breeding season by attaching a disinfected nest box onto the cage and enrich the diet. Be certain that the birds are at least one year old, are in excellent plumage, are not molting, and have been eating an enriched diet for at least four months prior to nesting. The enriched diet includes all of the feed and supplements of the maintenance diet and an increase in the amount of fresh greens daily. Offer the birds some soft vegetables to see if they are accepted. Some do and some don't enjoy vegetables, but it's worth trying. Fresh millet sprays should be supplied daily to breeding birds, especially when they are feeding their young. Millet spray is easily digested and can lessen the possibility of impacted crop.

Some parents are so enthusiastic about feeding their young that they tend to stuff them too full of hard seed; this can lead to impacted crops. Again the extra soft greens will help eliminate this, as will the suggested supplemental oils (cod liver or wheat germ).

Parakeet nesting boxes and cages are readily available at your local bird shop. Parakeets do not line their nests, so it is not necessary to provide nesting material as you would for larger parrots.

The birds will begin to investigate the box, which should ideally hang on the outside of the cage. If you do not disturb the birds too much, they should begin their natural breeding cycle within a few weeks, providing that you have healthy birds each a year or more older.

The normal clutch of eggs can be from four to six or seven. Different pairs produce a different number of young. Some hatch six chicks but raise only four. Don't be disappointed in your budgies if their first nests do not go well. Birds seem to need to practice a bit before they get the idea.

Babies remain in the nest for three and a half to four weeks before they venture out into the cage. They will quickly return to the nest if you approach and will roost in there for a few nights even after they emerge from the nest.

Opposite: *Breeding budgies is an enjoyable, challenging hobby for those with time, patience, and room. No budgie should be bred, however, unless it is in excellent condition.*

Left: *Budgerigars should never be left alone with other pets.*
Below: *Budgies should never be kept in cages meant to house macaws or cockatoos, as the spacing between the wires is large enough to allow the budgie to escape.*

Right: *One of the first things a new budgie owner should learn how to do is to pick up the bird properly. This will be helpful when the bird needs its claws clipped or needs to be examined for other reasons.* **Below:** *Never allow your budgie to chew on any plants unless you are sure they are not poisonous and have never been treated with chemicals.*

This is the ideal time to begin handling and taming a budgie. Remember that a four week old bird is not yet eating independently and must be returned to the parents for feedings unless you plan to do some hand feeding. I think that parent-reared young are more desirable because they grow faster, achieve a larger size, and do not become imprinted on humans (this would make them more difficult to mate up and breed in the future).

The baby budgie should be hand raised only if the natural parents refuse to feed it. Try fostering the neglected chick to another pair that is nesting, if possible. Usually if the new baby is placed in a nest with babies of

An opaline cobalt cock peeking out of its nesting box. The breeding pair will probably examine the box before the actual mating takes place.

An array of brightly colored budgies. This gives the prospective breeder an idea about the possibilities of budgie color breeding.

similar size, the foster parents will feed it automatically. Watch carefully to be certain that the fostered bird is fed. If it is not fed, pull it out, feed it and place it back into the nest with the others unless it is pecked or abused in other ways.

By taking advantage of the high heat and humidity in the nest, you can save yourself the trouble of trying to duplicate the best possible atmosphere for young nestlings.

Some parents are very gentle with their young, while others

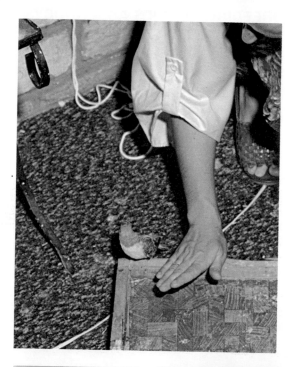

Left: *If your bird has had its wings clipped, it will have great difficulty in trying to escape while you are training it. The first step in hand training is to offer your hand to the bird for it to step on.*
Below: *If your budgie has not had its wings clipped, be sure to cover the windows; if the bird escapes from its cage, it will then be able to distinguish the window and will avoid flying into it.*

Right: *If you intend to breed budgies, they should be banded so that they can later be identified.* **Below:** *Never breed budgies during the molting period, as the loss of feathers at this time is stressful enough for the birds.*

Opposite top: *Headstudy of a male budgerigar.* **Opposite bottom:** *Headstudy of a female budgie. Note the difference in the colors of the cere.* **Above:** *Breeding pairs should consist of birds that have proven to be compatible.*

pluck out the youngsters' first fledgling feathers. When you have a pair that is consistently plucking the feathers from their young, you must examine the situation. Is there enough protein in the diet? Are the mineral and vitamin supplements provided in adequate doses?

When you encounter a pair of budgies that has an acquired vice for chewing their young, you should consider separating them. There is nothing to gain in raising young that are abused by their parents. Try to determine which parent is the aggressor and keep it separate from birds of the opposite sex. Repair the other bird and watch carefully to see if the abuse is repeated with a new mate.

Budgies should begin eating independently at five to six weeks

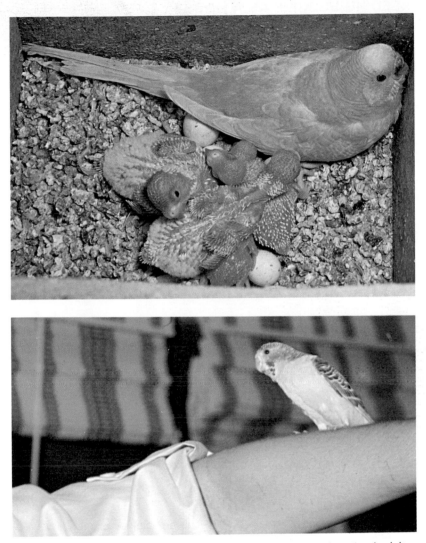

Opposite: *The author with one of her tame budgerigars.* **Top:** *A mother budgie with her brood of babies inside the nesting box.* **Bottom:** *You may wish to tame your baby budgies before selling them, as tame budgerigars fetch a higher price on the market.*

A grey green barhead cock budgerigar. Budgies should be at least one year old before they are bred.

and can be safely removed to a nursery cage at six weeks of age. Do not isolate the new baby. Place it with its siblings or with slightly older unaggressive budgies. In the nursery cage, the babies will become completely independent and within one week can be moved to a separate cage or sold as pets.

The breeding season usually begins in the fall and continues for three to four months. The summer months in hot climates are not good for breeding. The nest box gets too hot and the heat can be detrimental to the young and their parents. Allow your budgies to raise two to three clutches of young before interrupting the breeding season by removing the nest box and any eggs that the hen lays on the cage bottom. Allow your breeders to rest for at least four months before allowing them to breed again. Although some budgies will readily breed year round, you will eventually notice that the chicks are inferior compared to their older siblings.

If you must hand rear a bird, use warmed baby pablum and add some strained baby food green vegetables that are sold at the

A grey cock budgerigar. Budgies should not be allowed to raise more than two or three clutches in succession.

Opposite top and bottom: *The author with a hand tame budgie.* **Above:** *The amount of time spent in training the budgie is equal to the quality of that bird's quality as a pet.*

market. Always feed warm food to the youngsters, and consult an experienced person before beginning to hand rear. The first feedings for a very young budgie often must be given 24 hours a day. Feed the bird small amounts of liquified formula and thicken the formula as the baby grows. Try to get an accurate gram scale to weigh the chick every day to keep track of its weight gain or loss.

Begin to wean the baby at three to four weeks of age by placing formula in a dish within easy reach of the youngster. Also provide regular parakeet seed, millet spray and fresh greens. During weaning, be sure to fill the baby's crop before putting it to sleep for the night.

Budgie breeders should always strive for quality in their birds, not for quantity. Good birds will lead long and happy lives.

Index

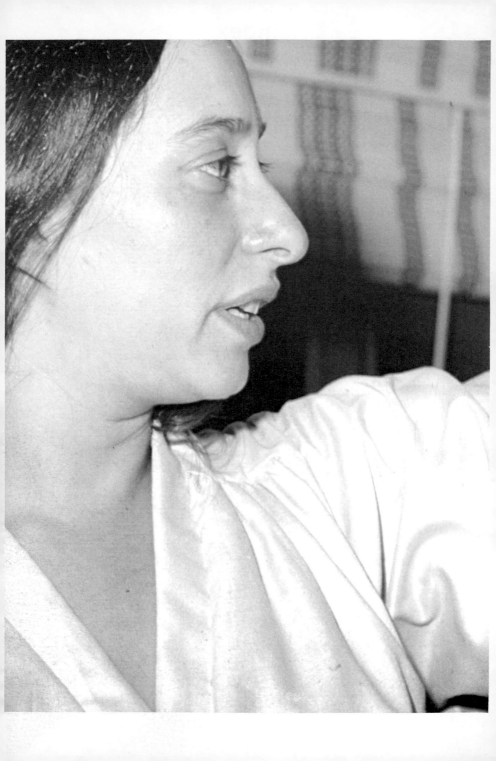

TAMING AND TRAINING YOUR
FIRST BUDGERIGAR
KW-070